SPICE

Decadent Recipes by
The Mistress of Spice

✳ ✳ ✳

Aparna Khanolkar

Acknowledgments

This book is dedicated to my most special students of 2011. Their interest, curiosity and commitment inspired me to teach cooking classes every Thursday evening from May to November. Special appreciation for Adam Cote, Eliza McEmrys, little Luke McEmrys, Mandy Pan and Jo Williams.

Respect and deep love to my parents Anand and Pushpa Khanolkar and my grandmother Sarojini Khanolkar for those special trips to the market and for teaching me about food and cooking. And to Mother Divine for all that I am.

Deep bows of gratitude for Rick Nagy and Elizabeth Messina.

Table of Contents

Spices

Many wars have been fought over spices. And many lands have been conquered for spices. Their value whether medicinal or taste has beckoned many from afar. In 1492 Christopher Columbus sailed to find India and spices. Instead he discovered the New World. Only five years later, Vasco Da Gama who was searching for a new spice route found India. It is said that his trip took two years and he brought back spices and other cargo that was worth more than 60 times the cost of the perilous voyage.

India has a rich offering of spices and her regional cooking proves it. There are over 80 spices of which 50 are grown in India. Spices are mentioned in 7,000 year- old Vedic texts. Black pepper, ginger, turmeric, chili, cardamom, fenugreek, cinnamon, fennel, cumin, ajwain or Bishop's weed, clove, coriander, clove, nutmeg and saffron are some of the spices that are grown in India. Spices are medicine – concentrated forms of intelligence from Mother Nature. Spices heal our body and mind, flavor food and transport us to realms of pure intoxication.

Indian food is a complex blend of curries, sauces and spice mixes. Each region offers its own variation on the theme called "masala." Masala means combination of spices, toasted and ground to a powder.

Spice blends are created for flavor but also carefully measured for they can balance the body and mind. In the summer you use spices such as coriander, fennel, and herbs such as dill and mint. In the winter, mustard seeds, ajwain and cumin create warmth in the body.

In these recipes, you will see different combinations of spices and herbs used in fish, vegetable and chicken dishes. When you use spices with meat, you are able to digest the meal more effectively. So, make friends with spices.

There are two ways to use spices.

- In powder form
- In seed form

In Indian cooking, both ways are used. When using it in powder form, make sure you dry toast the seeds in a small skillet on medium heat till fragrant – about 4-5 minutes. Don't walk away from it. Stir it often so it does not burn. Let it cool. Grind it in a coffee grinder and store in a cool, dark place. Use a separate coffee grinder for spices because their aromas are intense and will leave residual flavors in your coffee.

Spices lose their flavor and color when exposed to light and heat. Get a stainless steel spice box from Cost Plus World Market. Affordable and compact, it has seven containers. Every Indian household has one of these attractive boxes.

Not only will you enjoy the taste of spices in your food and the complex flavors in your mouth, you will also aid your digestive system. A common digestive aid served at the end of the meal is toasted fennel seeds. Cardamom is also a great breath freshener. Clove has been used for toothache while coriander for cooling an over-heated body.

Explore the world of spices through the recipes in this book. It will be tantamount to traveling to different regions of India. You will be pleased by the results.

Curries

If you have dined on curries at Indian restaurants and love the sauce flavors, then you are going to love cooking from this section. Indian restaurants in America tend to use too much oil and cream. You can create great Indian curries in your home without too much oil or cream. At home, use good quality grapeseed oil. The recipes below are from different regions of India. Each one of them are exquisitely delicious yet different. Some curries such as Vegetable Korma and Kashmiri Chicken Curry are from the North, others such as Kerala Fish Curry are from the South. Try them all and you will find your favorite flavors and go back time and time again to prepare it for you friends and family.

Coconut Curry with Mushrooms

Ingredients:

2 tbsp oil
½ onion cut into one inch chunks
½ tsp grated ginger
2 cloves of garlic finely chopped
½ tsp turmeric
1 tbsp coriander powder
½ tsp cumin powder
½ tsp cayenne
¾ tsp fennel powder
1 potato peeled and cut into one-inch chunks
1 carrot thinly sliced
6 shitake mushrooms
2 cans coconut milk
1 ½ tsp salt
½ tsp agave or sugar

Preparation:

Heat the oil in a large skillet. Add the onion and sauté for about 3-4 minutes. Now add the garlic and ginger and sauté for 45 seconds. Next add the spices, and the potatoes and sauté for about 4 minutes. Now add the other vegetables and sauté for 2 minutes. Add the coconut milk, salt and sugar and simmer for about 7-8 minutes or till the potatoes are tender. Serve with rice.

Vegetable Korma

Ingredients:

1 medium carrot thinly sliced
½ cup green beans cut into 1 inch pieces
1 small potato cut into 1 inch pieces
½ cup peas
½ cup water
3 tbsp oil
1 small onion finely chopped
1 Thai chili finely chopped

½ tsp grated ginger
1 clove of garlic finely chopped
2 tomatoes finely chopped
1 tsp garam masala (see recipe below)
5-7 cashews (soaked in ½ cup of hot water)
¼ cup cream or half and half
1 ½ tsp salt
paneer cubes 15 pieces

Preparation:

Place the vegetables and half the salt and the half cup of water in a medium sized pot and bring to a boil. Let it simmer for 3-4 minutes and turn the heat off and keep aside. In the meanwhile, add the oil to a skillet and fry the onions on medium heat till they are translucent. Do not brown the onions. Then add the chilies, ginger and garlic and cook for another 2-3 minutes. Add the tomatoes and cook on high heat till most of the moisture evaporates. Turn the heat down till the tomato mixture become thick. Add the vegetables, paneer, salt, garam masala and salt and mix well. Place the drained cashews and half and half in a blender and grind to a fine paste. Add this to the curry and simmer for 3-4 minutes. Serve with chapattis or rice.

Garam Masala:

Cumin seeds - 1 tsp
Coriander seeds - 1 tbsp
Pepper corns - 1 tsp
Cinnamon - 1 inch stick

Cardamom – 2 pods discard the pods and use only the seeds
2 cloves

Place all the spices in a dry skillet and toast on medium low heat till fragrant. Stir constantly. When cool, place in a spice grinder and grind to a fine powder. Store in a jar and use in curries.

Palak Paneer

Ingredients:

½ cup cubed paneer
Boil together in ¼ cup of water only until the spinach wilts:
1 ½ lb baby spinach
1-2 Roma tomatoes cut in ½
2 Thai chilies

Spices:

Dry toast and grind to a powder in a spice grinder.
½ tsp cumin seeds
1 clove
Seeds from one cardamom pod
6-8 cashews

For the final step:

3 tbsp oil
½ tsp cumin seeds
1 tsp grated ginger
1 clove of garlic finely chopped

1 ½ tsp salt

Preparation:

Place all the vegetables in a blender and grind coarsely. Keep aside. After dry toasting the spices, grind along with cashews to a fine powder and keep aside. Now, heat oil in a pan and add the cumin seeds. Once they sizzle, add the ginger and garlic and sauté for about 45 seconds. Add the ground spinach, paneer, salt and the spices with cashews and simmer for about 4-5 minutes. Serve with pooris and rice.

Kerala Fish Curry

For masala:

Ingredients:

1 tbsp coriander seeds
1 clove
½ tsp fennel seeds
½ tsp crushed red pepper
Seeds from one cardamom pod
One half inch of a cinnamon stick
½ tsp peppercorns

1 tbsp grapeseed oil
1 tbsp cider vinegar
2 tsp grated ginger
1 large clove of garlic finely chopped
¾ tsp turmeric
½ tsp salt

For the fish:

3 tbsp oil
10 fresh curry leaves
2 cloves of garlic finely chopped
1 large onion thinly sliced
½ inch ginger cut into matchsticks

1 cup chopped tomatoes
1 lb of fish cut into 2 inch pieces such as halibut or salmon
¾ tsp salt

Preparation:

For the masala:

In a mortar and pestle or spice grinder, grind the following spices to a powder:

Coriander, cardamom, clove, fennel, red pepper, cinnamon and peppercorns.

Transfer to a small bowl and mix the oil, vinegar and salt in and keep aside.

In a large skillet, heat the oil and add the curry leaves. Cook for about 30 seconds and add the onions, garlic and ginger. Cook for about 7-8 minutes or till the onions are soft. Add the masala paste and cook till it is fragrant. Now add the tomatoes and cook till it is soft and becomes thick. Now add the fish and salt. Mix gently and cook on low heat till the fish is cooked through. You may need ½ cup of water, if the sauce is too thick. Serve with rice.

Note: Curry leaves are available at Indian grocers.

Punjabi Chicken Curry

Ingredients:

3 tbsp oil
1 large onion finely chopped
1 tbsp crushed garlic
1 tbsp grated ginger
1 tsp turmeric
¾ tsp cayenne
3 Roma tomatoes finely chopped
3 chicken breasts into one inch cubes
1 ½ tsp salt

Preparation:

Heat oil in a large pot and add the onions and fry on medium heat till the onions are golden brown. If you rush this step the onions will brown on the outside and remain crunchy on the inside. By taking the time to cook the onions, you will have imparted a sweet flavor to the curry. Now add the garlic, ginger, turmeric and cayenne and mix well. Cook for 2-3 minutes. Next add the tomatoes and increase the heat to high. Cook the tomatoes till all the moisture evaporates and the mixture is thick. Now add the chicken and salt and mix well. Cover with a tight-fitting lid. Cook on low heat till the chicken is completely cooked about 25-30 minutes. Serve with pooris or rice.

Chicken Masala Curry

Ingredients:

5 tbsp oil
2 medium onions finely chopped
1 small bulb of garlic finely chopped
1 tbsp grated ginger
1 tsp turmeric
1 tsp cumin powder
2 tbsp coriander powder
¼ tsp cinnamon powder
1/8 tsp clove powder
½ tsp cayenne
3 tbsp tomato paste
5 chicken thighs
2 tsp salt
¾ cup of water
4 ounces of heavy cream

Preparation:

Heat oil in a large pot. Add the onions and cook on medium heat till golden brown. Now add the ginger and garlic. Cook for 2 minutes. Add the spice powders. Mix well. Now add the tomato paste and chicken and cook on high heat for 3-4 minutes. Add the salt and water and bring to a boil. Now, turn the heat down, cover with a tight-fitting lid and cook on low heat for 30 minutes or till the chicken pieces are cooked through. Now add the cream and simmer for 3-4 minutes. Serve hot with rice or chapattis.

Kashmiri Chicken Curry

Ingredients:

3 tbsp oil
2 bay leaves
3 whole cloves
1 small onion thinly sliced
½ tsp grated ginger
1 clove of garlic finely chopped
½ tsp turmeric
1 tsp cumin powder
¼ tsp cinnamon
¼ tsp cardamom
½ tsp cayenne
3 chicken breasts cut into one inch cubes
1 can coconut milk
½ cup water
2 tsp salt
8-10 cashews ground to a fine powder

Preparation:

Heat the oil and add the bay leaves and cloves. Cook for 45 seconds. Now add the onion and cook on medium heat for about 10-12 minutes. It is very important to have the onions become translucent versus brown as this will discolor the sauce. Now add the ginger, garlic, turmeric, cinnamon, cardamom and cayenne. Mix well and cook for one minute. Add the chicken and turn the heat up to high for 3 minutes. Now add the coconut milk, water and salt and mix well. Cover with a tight-fitting lid and cook for 20 minutes on low heat. In the meanwhile, get the cashew powder ready. After cooking the chicken for 20 minutes, add the cashew powder and mix well and simmer for another 3-4 minutes. Serve with rice and naan.

Goan Fish Curry

Ingredients:

1 cup shredded coconut (fresh or frozen unsweetened Lakshmi brand)
¼ of a small onion
1 tsp coriander seeds
½ tsp turmeric
¾ tsp cayenne or more if you want it spicier
¾ cup of water
1 tbsp oil
¼ of a small onion finely chopped
2 fillets of white fish such as talapia, halibut, snapper or rock fish cut into 1 inch cubes (approximately 1 1/2 lbs)
1 small piece of tamarind (soaked in 3 tbsp of hot water)

Preparation:

Grind all the ingredients – from coconut to water. In the meanwhile, heat the oil in a medium-sized pot and add the onions and cook on medium low heat till golden brown. Turn the heat down and add the coconut paste to the onions. Squeeze the tamarind pulp with your fingers and add the water to the curry. Discard the fiber and seeds. Mix well and cook on low heat to avoid curdling the coconut. Simmer this sauce for about 7-8 minutes. Add the fish pieces and mix gently and place a lid on the pot and cook till the fish is done. The cooking time depends on the kind of fish you use in this curry. Serve with rice.

Spicy Green Chicken Curry

Ingredients:

4-6 tbsp oil
2 tsp cumin seeds
2 large onions thinly sliced
1 tbsp grated ginger
4 large clove of garlic finely chopped
1 ½ tsp turmeric
2 lb bone-in chicken cut up into small pieces

For the Sauce:

1 big bunch of cilantro
1 bunch of mint (leaves only)
4 whole cloves
6 Thai chilies
½ tsp cinnamon powder
1/4 cup water
2 tsp salt

Preparation:

Heat oil in a large pot and add the cumin seeds. Fry it for about 40 seconds and add the onions. Cook in high heat for about 3-4 minutes. Now turn the heat down and cook on medium heat for about 10 minutes. Then add the ginger and garlic and mix well. Cook for 3-4 minutes. Add the turmeric and chicken and turn the heat up to high for about 3 minutes. Stir frequently. In the meanwhile, place all the sauce ingredients in the blender and grind to a smooth paste and add to the chicken. Mix well to coat the chicken pieces with the sauce. Place a tight-fitting lid and cook on low heat for 30 minutes. Cooking the curry on low heat is essential in making sure the chicken is tender. Serve with cumin rice.

Paneer Masala

Ingredients:

For the Masala:

3 tbsp oil
1 tsp cumin seeds
1 small onion finely chopped
1 tsp finely chopped garlic
1 tsp grated ginger
½ tsp turmeric
2 tsp coriander powder
¼ tsp cinnamon
¼ tsp clove powder
3 Roma tomatoes finely chopped
¼ tsp cayenne powder
½ tsp sugar
1 ½ tsp salt
½ cup water
1 cup paneer cubes
2 tbsp finely chopped cilantro

Paneer:

1 gallon organic whole milk
Juice of 3 limes

Preparation:

Bring the milk to a boil in a large pot and slowly add the lime juice while stirring constantly. After the whey and curd separate, strain in a colander layered with cheese cloth and place something heavy, such as a cast-iron skillet and allow it to compact. Let the paneer rest for about 25 minutes. Remove the cheese cloth and cut into half inch cubes. In the meanwhile, heat the oil in a large pot and add the cumin, onion, ginger and garlic. Sauté on medium heat for 6-8 minutes or till the onions are soft. Now add all the spice powders except cayenne and sauté for about 45 seconds. Then add the tomatoes and cook till thick. Add the sugar, salt and cayenne and simmer for about 10 minutes. Now add the paneer and mix gently. Simmer for another 4 minutes. Just before serving add the cilantro.

Chettinadu Chicken Curry

Ingredients:

3 tbsp of oil
1 tbsp mustard seeds
2 tbsp fennel seeds
20 curry leaves
2 cinnamon sticks
5 cardamom pods crushed
1 large onion finely chopped
1 tbsp finely chopped garlic
1 tbsp grated ginger
1 tsp turmeric
1 tsp cumin powder
2 tbsp coriander powder
4 Roma tomatoes (ground to a puree in a blender)
2 tbsp black pepper
6 thighs of chicken (boneless skinless)
10 oz of frozen coconut (finely ground with one cup of water)
2 ½ tsp salt
4 tbsp finely chopped cilantro leaves

Preparation:

Heat the oil and add the mustard seeds and allow them to pop. Once they seeds pop, add the curry leaves, fennel seeds, cinnamon, cardamom and onions and cook on medium low heat for 5-8 minutes or till the onions are golden brown. Now add the garlic and ginger and cook for another 2 minutes. Add the spice powders and tomatoes and cook for 8-10 minutes or till all the moisture evaporates and the tomato sauce is thick. Now add the chicken, salt and pepper and cook for 4-5 minutes. Add the ground coconut and 1 cup of water and simmer on medium low heat for 30 minutes. Garnish with cilantro and serve with rice.

Bombay Chicken Curry

Ingredients:

4 tbsp oil
2 medium onions finely chopped
3 Thai chilies finely chopped
3 tbsp finely chopped garlic
1 tbsp grated ginger

4 tomatoes finely chopped
2 1/2 lb chicken bone-in, skin removed and cut into 4 inch pieces
2-3 tsp salt
1 can coconut milk

For masala:

3 tbsp oil
2 medium onions thinly sliced
20 whole peppercorns
2 tbsp white poppy seeds
4 whole cloves
2 inch piece cinnamon
1 tbsp fennel seeds

2 tbsp coriander seeds
1 star anise
1 cup fresh grated coconut (or buy frozen at Indian grocers – Lakshmi brand is best)
1 cup of water

Preparation:

In a large pot, heat the oil and add the finely chopped onions. Cook on medium heat till light brown. Now add the Thai chili, garlic and ginger. Cook on 2-3 minutes and then add tomatoes. Turn the heat up to medium high and cook till the moisture evaporates. Then turn the heat down and cook till it turns thick and lumpy. Now add the chicken and salt and cook on high heat for 5-8 minutes. Keep aside. In the meanwhile, heat a skillet and add 3 tbsp oil, onions, poppy seeds and spices. Cook on medium heat for 5-6 minutes stirring often so the spices do not burn.

Now add the coconut and continue cooking while stirring often so the coconut does not burn. When the mixture is cool, place the masala ingredients along with the water in a blender and grind to a fine paste. Add the ground masala paste to the chicken and turn the heat to high. When it begins boiling, ad the canned coconut milk and turn the heat to low and place a tight-fitting lid and cook for 30 minutes. Turn the pieces over once and cook it for 2-5 more minutes to ensure that the pieces are cooked through. Serve with lime wedges and red onion slices, rice and pooris.

Street Foods

Street foods are popular in every part of India. Take a walk down any busy city street after 5 p.m. and you are sure to be tantalized by the wafting aromas of pakoras, chaats and other regional delicacies. You will see men standing in front of large woks frying up treats to be purchased and eaten on the spot. These gluten free savory delights vary from region to region. The chickpea flour and the vegetables are common ingredients. You can re-create these dishes right in your kitchen.

Onion Pakoras

Ingredients:

1 cup besan (chickpea flour)
½ cup rice flour
2-3 Thai chilies finely chopped
½ tsp turmeric
2 large onions, sliced
¼ cup chopped cilantro
1 ½ tsp salt
A pinch of baking soda
Oil for deep frying

Preparation:

In a large mixing bowl, combine both the flours with salt, soda, Thai chilies, turmeric, onions and cilantro. Keep aside for 20 minutes so the salt releases water. After 20 minutes, if there is not enough moisture in the batter, add a few tbsps of water and mix with you hands. Heat 3 inches oil in a wok. Use your fingers to drop the batter in the oil to form small fritters. Reduce heat to medium high and deep fry till they turn golden brown. Use a slotted spoon to keep turning the fritters so that they cook on all sides. Once they turn golden brown, drain on paper towels and serve hot.

Pan-fried Shrimp

Ingredients:

8-12 large shrimp peeled, deveined and de-frosted
3/4 tsp turmeric
3/4 tsp cayenne
1 1/4 tsp salt
3-4 tbsp oil for cooking
5 tbsp semolina for dredging

Preparation:

In a small bowl, mix the well-drained shrimp along with turmeric, cayenne and salt. Marinade for 15 minutes. Heat oil in a small skillet. As the oil is heating, dredge the shrimp in the semolina, making sure that all parts of the shrimp are coated evenly. Now place the shrimp in the oil and cook for about two minutes on each side. Drain on paper towels. Serve immediately.

Aloo Bondas

Ingredients:

For the filling:

2 large potatoes	½ inch ginger grated
2 tbsp oil	1/2 tsp turmeric
1 tsp mustard seeds	3 tbsp chopped cilantro
½ tsp urad dal	2 tsp salt
1 tsp of cumin powder	Juice of 1 lime
3 Thai chilies chopped finely	

For the Batter:

3/4 cup Besan flour (chickpea flour)	A pinch of hing (asafetida)
1/2 cup of water or a bit more	A pinch of baking soda
½ tsp cayenne	2 cups of oil for deep frying

Preparation:

For the Filling;

Boil the potatoes in 2 quarts of water till they are tender. Peel and mash with a fork and keep aside. In a large pot, heat the oil and add the mustard seeds. After they pop add the urad dal, chilies and ginger. Cook for about 15 seconds. Then add the turmeric, potatoes. And salt. Remove from heat and mix well. Allow it to cool and when it is lukewarm form them into small balls and keep aside.

Mix all the batter ingredients together except for the oil and keep aside. Heat the oil and dip the potato ball carefully in the batter and allow for excess to fall back into the bowl. Carefully place a few batter -coated potato balls into the hot oil. Use a tablespoon to dip the potato balls in the batter. This gives it an even coating and makes it easy to place in the oil. Fry them till golden brown on all sides. Drain on paper towels and serve immediately or place on a cookie sheet on a single layer and warm in a 250 degree oven for 15 minutes before serving. Serve with chutney.

Bell Pepper Pakoras

Ingredients:

2 green pepper seeded and cut into 2 inch strips
2 cups of oil for frying

Batter:

1 cup besan (chickpea flour)
½ tsp turmeric
1 tsp salt
1 tbsp dried fenugreek leaves (optional)
1 tsp fennel powder
1 tsp coriander powder
½ cup water for mixing and add as needed to have the consistency of a slightly runny pancake batter

Preparation:

Heat oil in a large wok. While the oil heats, mix all the ingredients for the coating. Place a small amount of the batter into the oil and if it sizzles and rises to the surface immediately, the oil is ready for frying. Dip the vegetables and carefully place in the hot oil in a single layer without crowding. Fry on medium heat for about 5 minutes on each side. Drain on paper towels and serve immediately.

Alternatives:

Small cauliflower and broccoli florets, thinly sliced potatoes, individual spinach leaves all make great fritters.

Savory Corn Fritters

Ingredients:

1 cob of corn kernels removed with a sharp knife
1 medium onion thinly sliced
1 clove of garlic finely chopped
½ bunch cilantro finely chopped
½ tsp turmeric
1 tsp salt
½- ¾ cup of chickpea flour
1 tsp fennel powder
¼ tsp cayenne powder
A sprinkling of water if necessary
2 cups of oil for frying

Preparation:

With a sharp knife, slice the corn kernels from the cob into a large bowl. Add the onion, garlic, cilantro, turmeric, salt, chickpea flour, fennel, and cayenne and mix well. If the dough is very dry, sprinkle a few teaspoons of water and let it sit for 10 minutes. Then heat the oil in a medium-sized wok and re-mix the dough. To test the oil, carefully drop a tiny bit of the batter into the oil. If the batter sizzles and rises to the surface immediately, the oil is ready. Add 1 tsp of the dough at a time into the oil. Do not crowd the wok or else the oil will cool down. If the oil cools down it will be absorbed into the fritters. Fry on one side for 2-3 minutes or till golden brown and then turn the fritters over and fry on the other side for another 2 minutes or so. Drain on paper towels and serve immediately with cilantro chutney.

Kebabs

Kebabs are a popular dish in North India. It is a delicious testimony to the marriage of Middle Eastern and Indian cuisine. If you visit the narrow, crowded streets of Old Delhi, you can sample many types of delicate kebabs. Although cooking these in a tandoor clay oven is best for succulent morsels of kebabs, you can use the oven quite successfully as well. You can also use your BBQ. Serve with naan, chutney, slices of red onion and wedges of lime.

Minted Chicken Kebabs

Ingredients:

1.5 lbs of ground chicken
30 leaves of mint finely chopped
4 Thai chilies finely chopped
½ small onion finely chopped
1 tbsp grated ginger
3 cloves of garlic finely chopped
1 tsp turmeric
1 ½ tsp salt
1 bunch cilantro leaves only finely chopped
Oil for cooking

Preparation:

Mix all the ingredients together except for the oil. Keep aside for 20 minutes. Heat a cast iron skillet and add 2 tbsp of oil. Wet your hands with water and form 1 inch balls and gently add to the skillet. Cook on medium low heat till the kebabs are fully cooked, turning often. If cooking in the oven, place the kebabs on an oiled baking tray and bake at 300 degrees till cooked through about 25-30 minutes. If you wish to BBQ, soak 10 skewers in warm water for 20 minutes. Take a handful of the kebab mixture and gently pack the meat around the skewers, forming a 4-inch long sausage shape on each skewer. Grill on medium heat till cooked through.

Chicken Tikka

Ingredients:

1 1/2 lbs boneless skinless chicken breasts cut into 1" cubes
1/3 cup yogurt
1 1/2 tbsp grated ginger
1 tbsp garlic
1 tsp chilli powder
1 tbsp coriander powder
1 1/2 tsp salt
Juice of one lemon
1 tbsp oil

Preparation:

Mix all ingredients in a bowl, except the chicken and blend well. Add the chicken cubes and marinade overnight or 3 - 4 hours. Soak 6 bamboo skewers in warm water for 20 minutes. Divide the chicken pieces equally into 6 portions and thread them on to skewers. Barbeque or grill on medium low heat till cooked. If baking, preheat oven to 350 degrees and bake for 12-15 minutes or until chicken is cooked and browned lightly. Turn frequently, particularly on the barbeque. Serve with chutney and Cumin Scented Basmati Rice.

Tandoori Chicken

Ingredients:

4 -6 chicken thighs (bone-in)
½ cup yogurt
1 ½ tsp salt
The juice of one lime
5 cloves garlic crushed
1 tsp grated ginger
2 Thai chilies
1 tsp black pepper corns
2 cardamom pods
1 tsp cumin seeds
1/2 tsp nutmeg powder
¼ cinnamon stick
4 cloves
1 tsp paprika

Preparation:

Grind the onion, green chilies, ginger and garlic together with half the yogurt. Dry grind all the spices to a fine powder and keep aside. Place the chicken in a bowl and add the ground onion mixture as well as the dry spice powders and mix well. Add the remaining yogurt and marinade overnight. Pre-heat the oven to 275 degrees and place the chicken in a baking tray and cook for 20 minutes. After 20 minutes, turn the chicken pieces over and cook for another 20 minutes. Serve hot with lime and red onion slices and naan.

Shammi Kebab

Ingredients:

1 ½ lbs ground lamb
1 tbsp grated ginger
4-5 cloves garlic crushed
¼ cup chana dal (Dry chana dal is available at your local Indian grocers)
1 egg
2-3 green chilies
2 tbsp chopped cilantro
1 tbsp chopped mint leaves
Juice of one lime
½ tsp garam masala powder (See Vegetable Korma recipe)
1 ½ tsp salt
Oil for cooking the kebabs

Preparation:

Wash the chana dal and add 2 cups of water and bring to a boil. Cook on medium heat till tender but not over cooked. Drain the cooked dal completely and grind coarsely without adding any water. Mix in with all the ingredients. Wet your hands and form small patties. Heat a cast iron skillet and add 1 tbsp of oil. Add a single layer of patties and cook on medium heat till well browned on both sides. Serve with cilantro chutney.

Tangdi Kebab

Ingredients:

4-5 chicken drumsticks skin removed
1 ½ tsp salt
1 tsp finely chopped garlic
1 tsp grated ginger
The juice of one lime
½ small onion
5-7 stems of cilantro
½ tsp turmeric
5-8 whole peppercorns
1 Thai chili
¼ cup yogurt

Preparation:

Place the chicken in a bowl. Blend the onion along with the cilantro, ginger, garlic, lime juice, turmeric, peppercorns and Thai chili. Add this ground paste to the chicken along with yogurt. Marinate overnight. Cook on a grill or BBQ or roast in an oven at 500 degrees for 15-25 minutes or till cooked through. Turn at least once during cooking.

Fried Goan Fish

Ingredients:

1 ½ lb fish such as halibut, orange roughy or red snapper cut into 3 inch chunks
1 tsp turmeric
1 tsp grated ginger
2 cloves of garlic finely chopped
¾ tsp cayenne
1 ¼ tsp salt
Oil for frying

For dredging:

½ cup semolina

Preparation:

In a medium sized bowl, mix the fish, turmeric, ginger, garlic, cayenne and salt. Use your hands for mixing so the fish pieces are evenly coated with the marinade. Marinade for 4 hours or over night in the fridge. Heat a skillet and add 3-4 tbsp of oil, carefully dredge each piece of fish on each side in the semolina. Cook on medium heat till brown on one side, flip and cook on the other side. Serve immediately.

Rice

Rice is the staff of life in South India. I grew up in a town surrounded by rice growing paddies. Driving past lush paddies and watching women and men work on their land is still one of my fondest memories. Easy to cook and digest, rice is a great source of energy. An entire meal can be created with rice as in the Biryani recipe in this section. It is a versatile grain that willingly absorbs any flavor you add. You can substitute brown rice in any of these dishes. Just be aware of different cooking times for brown rice. These rice dishes below are some of my most favorite ones. I hope they will be yours too.

Vegetable Pulao

Ingredients:

1 ½ cups of white basmati rice
2 ¾ cups of water
1 ½ tsp salt
4 tbsp oil
2 bay leaves
2 cinnamon sticks
3 cardamom pods
2 Thai chilies
1 tsp cumin seeds
15 green beans ends trimmed and cut into 2 inch pieces
1 medium carrot thinly sliced
½ small cabbage thinly shredded
1 red pepper cut into 1 inch pieces
3/4 tsp salt

Preparation:

Wash the rice in three changes of water and drain completely. Add the washed rice, measured water and salt to a medium sized pot and bring to a rapid boil. Now place a tight-fitting lid on the pot and cook on low heat for 15 minutes. Turn the heat off and let it sit for 5 minutes. While the rice cools, heat oil in a large skillet and add the whole spices. Cook for 45 seconds. Now add the chilies, vegetables and salt. Cook on high heat for 4 minutes to get the vegetables colorful. Add the cooked rice and carefully fold the rice into the vegetables to avoid breaking the grains of rice. Serve hot with chicken curry or vegetable korma.

Cumin Scented Basmati Rice

Ingredients:

2 tbsp oil
1 tsp cumin seeds
1 medium onion thinly sliced
1 ½ cups of white Basmati rice
1 ½ tsp salt
2 ¾ cups of water

Preparation:

Wash the rice in three changes of water. Drin completely and keep aside. Heat the oil in a medium sized pot and add the oil and cumin seeds. When the cumin seeds sizzle, add the onions and cook on medium heat till they turn light brown. Now add the washed and drained rice and salt and stir fry gently for about 2-3 minutes. Add the water and bring to a rapid boil. Now place a tight-fitting lid and turn the heat down to low and cook for 15 minutes. Let the rice sit for 5 minutes before serving.

Chicken Pulao

Ingredients:

5 tbsp oil
3 bay leaves
2 tsp cumin seeds
4 cardamom pods
1 star anise
1 black cardamom
4 whole cloves
2 medium onions
1 tsp grated ginger
4 cloves of garlic finely chopped
4 tomatoes finely chopped
1 tsp cayenne
1 1/2 lbs of bone-in cut up chicken –skin removed
1 ½ cups of white Basmati rice
2 1/4 cups of water
3 ½ tsp salt
4 tbsp chopped cilantro
Lime wedges

Preparation:

Heat the oil in a large pot and add the bay leaves, cumin seeds, cardamom pods, star anise, black cardamom and cloves and cook for 45 seconds or till they sizzle. Next, add the onions and cook on medium heat till they are light brown. Now add the ginger and garlic and cook for 3-4 minutes. Add the tomatoes and cayenne and turn the heat up to high. Cook till the moisture evaporates and a thick paste is formed. Now add the chicken and cook for 3-4 minutes, stirring often. Next add the rice, water and salt and bring to a boil. If you have a rice cooker, transfer the rice and chicken to the cooker and cook till done. If not, bring the chicken, rice and water to a rapid boil. Now place a tight-fitting lid and turn the heat down to low and cook for 15-17 minutes. Sprinkle with cilantro and serve with lime wedges.

Chicken Biryani

Ingredients:

For roasting:

3 large onions thinly sliced
2 tbsp oil

For Chicken:

4 tbsp oil	8 large cloves of garlic finely chopped
2 tsp cumin seeds	3 tbsp coriander powder
5 dry red chilies broken into pieces	1 tsp cayenne
1 tsp whole peppercorns	2 lbs of bone-in chicken, skin
5 whole cloves	removed and cut into 4 inch pieces
5 cardamom pods	¼ cup of plain yogurt
1 large onion thinly sliced	2 tsp salt

For rice:

2 cups Basmati rice	2 cardamom pods
1 tsp cumin seeds	1 ½ tsp salt
4 whole cloves	3 cups water

Preparation:

Pre-heat oven to 300 degrees. On a baking tray, mix the onions and oil and roast till they are caramelized – about 40 minutes. Keep aside. In the meanwhile, heat a wok or large skillet and add the oil and add the cumin seeds, red chilies, peppercorns, whole cloves, cardamom pods and the onion. Cook on medium heat till the onions are light brown. Next add the garlic, chicken, salt, coriander powder and cayenne. Mix well and let it cook for 2 minutes. Now add the yogurt and mix well. Place a tight-fitting lid and cook on medium heat for about 5-8 minutes. By then, a thick sauce should develop in the pan with the chicken. If not, cook for another two minutes or so.

In the meanwhile, wash the rice in three changes of water and drain completely. Draining the rice thoroughly is a very essential step. Too much water will make your biryani mushy. Place the washed rice, measured water, spices and salt in a large rice cooker and add the chicken pieces to it. Mix well, cover with the lid and cook till done. Let it sit for 10 minutes and fold very gently to mix. Serve with raitha.

Bombay Shrimp Pulao

Ingredients:

1 1/2 cups basmati rice (washed and drained completely)
2 1/2 cups water
1 1/4 tsp salt
4 tbsp oil
2 cinnamon sticks
4 cardamom pods
4 cloves
1/2 tsp ajwain seeds
1 tsp cumin seeds
3 bay leaves
1/2 tsp whole peppercorns
3 Thai chilies slit lengthwise
½ tsp turmeric
1 medium onion thinly sliced
1 tsp grated ginger
2 cloves of garlic finely chopped

Shrimp marinade:

1/2 tsp cayenne
1/2 tsp turmeric
1/2 tsp salt
1.5 lb of shrimp deveined and *peeled*

Preparation:

Heat oil in a medium pot. Add the whole spices and cook for 45 seconds. Now add the onions, turmeric and chilies and cook on medium low heat till soft and light brown. Add the ginger and garlic and cook for 1 minute. Add the washed and drained rice and salt and saute for 3-4 minutes. Now add the water and bring to a rapid boil. Add the marinated shrimp and place a tight-fitting lid on the pot and cook on low heat on for 15 minutes. Garnish with fresh coconut, cilantro and lime wedges.

Chutneys and Raitha

Chutneys and raitha are important accompaniments to an Indian meal. The different flavors of the chutneys not only taste good, but also aid digestion. Raithas are cooling and lend balance to spicy curries. Chutneys and raitha add color and flair to your party. You and your guests will love the different tastes and digestive benefits of these fresh and simple condiments.

Mint Cilantro Chutney

Ingredients:

2 bunches of cilantro
1 bunch of fresh mint, leaves only
2 Thai chilies
1 clove garlic
1 inch ginger root, chopped
½ tsp cumin powder
¾ tsp sugar
1 tsp. salt
2 tsp lime juice

Preparation:

Place all the ingredients in a blender. Add only a small quantity of water (about 1/8 cup at the most)and blend until smooth. This will keep in the fridge for 3-4 days.

Onion chutney

Ingredients:

1 tbsp oil
1 tsp mustard seeds
2 tsp urad dal divided (available at the local Indian grocers)
2 medium onions coarsely chopped
2 Thai chilies
One ½ inch piece of tamarind
½ tsp salt
½ tsp turbinado sugar

Preparation:

Heat the oil in a skillet and add the mustard seeds. Place a lid on the skillet and allow the seeds to pop. When they stop popping, add 1 tsp of the urad dal. Cook for 45 seconds and keep aside. In another skillet, heat another tbsp of oil and add the onions, the remaining tsp of urad dal and chilies and fry on medium heat till it turns golden brown. It is important that you don't cook the onions on high heat. Otherwise, you will have a raw taste in your chutney. Soak the tamarind in 1 tbsp of hot water and keep aside for 4 -5 minutes. Next squeeze the soaked tamarind and get all the pulp you can. Discard the seeds and fibers. When the onions are cooked, place them in a blender along with the tamarind, salt and turbinado sugar and blend to a fine paste. Transfer the chutney to a bowl, and add the popped mustard seeds and mix well. Serve at room temperature.

Garlic Chutney

Ingredients:

1/3 cup peeled garlic cloves sliced
1 cup dry shredded unsweetened coconut
4 tbsp black peppercorns
3 tbsp coriander seeds
1 ½ tsp salt
The juice of 1 lime
4 tbsp ghee (clarified butter)

Preparation:

Heat 2 tbsp of the ghee in a skillet on medium heat and add the garlic cloves. Fry it on medium heat for about 6minutes. When it has cooled, grind the garlic in a blender along with the rest of the ingredients to a fine paste. Add a little water for ease in grinding. Heat the rest of the ghee and add the ground paste and fry on medium heat for about 12 minutes. This ensures that the garlic is cooked and the moisture has evaporated. This chutney can be stored in the fridge for 3-5 days.

Raitha

Ingredients:

1 small cucumber
1.5 cups of plain yogurt
½ tsp cumin powder
1 tsp salt
½ tsp turbinado sugar
2 tbsp chopped cilantro

Preparation:

Peel and seed the cucumber. Finely chop or grate the cucumber into a medium sized bowl. Add the remaining ingredients and mix well and chill before serving.

Onion Raitha

Ingredients:

1 small red onion
1.5 cups of plain yogurt
½ tsp cumin powder
1 tsp salt
½ tsp turbinado sugar
2 tbsp chopped cilantro

Preparation:

Peel and slice the red onion very thinly. Place the onions and the other ingredients in a bowl and mix well. Chill before serving.

Lassis

Although Lassis are a very popular drink in the U.S, most restaurants add to much sugar and cream. At home, you can make a healthy yet decadent version. The Cumin Mint Lassi and the Rose Lassi are wonderful for the summer season because they quench thirst while cooling the body.

Mango Lassi

Ingredients:

¾ cup frozen mango chunks or 1 whole ripe sweet mango cut into chunks
2 tbsp cane sugar
2 cups 2% milk
1 tsp cardamom powder
4 cubes of ice (optional)

Preparation:

Place all the ingredients in a large blender such as Vitamix and blend on high till smooth. If you don't have a Vita-mix, run in a regular blender in two batches. Serve cold.

Rose Lassi

Ingredients:

16 oz plain yogurt
3 tbsp food grade rose water
½ tsp cardamom powder
¾ cup water
3 tbsp turbinado sugar

Preparation:

Place all ingredients in a blender and blend. Serve immediately.

Cumin Mint Lassi

Ingredients:

16 oz plain yogurt
1 tsp cumin powder
3/4 cup water
1 1/2 tsp salt
10 leaves of mint

Preparation:

Place all ingredients in a blender and blend. Serve immediately.

Breads

Wheat grows abundantly in North India, which makes bread a staple food. Simply speaking, breads are made with flour, oil, water and sometimes a few spices. The dough is mixed fresh, allowed to rest for about 20 minutes and then rolled out into the most delicious breads. There is no yeast, no preservatives and it is made just at meal times. Add **a** smear of ghee and you are eating the healthiest bread.

Poori

Poori – A deep fried bread that is most popular in India. Serve with any of the curries in this book.

Yield: 10 pooris

Ingredients:

1 cup whole wheat flour (pastry)
1/2 cup hot water
1/2 tsp salt
2 tsp oil
2 cups oil for deep frying

Preparation:

Mix the flour and salt. Add water as needed to make firm dough. Pour the 2 tsp of oil on the dough and knead well – about 4-5 minutes. The dough for poori should be firm but smooth. Set the dough aside and cover with a damp cloth. Let the dough rest for 15 minutes. Divide the dough in 10 equal parts. Take a few drops of oil on your palm and roll the dough in balls and press it between your palms to form round patties. Roll the dough evenly into about 6-inch disks. If the dough is sticking to the rolling pin or rolling surface, smear a couple of drops of oil on the rolling pin and a couple of drops of oil on the surface for ease in rolling.

You can roll 4 to 5 pooris before you start frying, but do not roll all the pooris at once or they will begin to dry and not puff. Heat the oil in a frying pan on medium high heat. To check if oil is hot enough place a small piece of dough in the oil. If the oil is ready, the dough will float to the top right away. If not, let it heat up for another 2 minutes or so.

Place one poori at a time in the frying pan and press it gently with a slotted spoon. The poori should puff right away. Turn the poori over. It should be light brown on both sides. Drain the poori on paper towels. Serve immediately.

Gobi Parathas

Parathas are stuffed breads. There are numerous stuffed bread dishes, which include ground chicken, paneer, radish, spinach and other vegetables. This cauliflower stuffed bread is simple and fool-proof.

Yield: 6 parathas

Ingredients:

Dough:

1 cup whole-wheat flour (pastry flour is best)
1/2 cup hot water (Use more as needed)
1/2 tsp of salt

Filling:

2 cups shredded cauliflower (you must grate by hand with a box grater not a food processor)
½ tsp turmeric
1 tsp fennel powder
1 tsp coriander powder
1/2 tsp cumin powder
1 Thai chili finely chopped
2 tbsp chopped cilantro
1 tsp salt

Also needed:

1/4 cup whole-wheat flour for rolling
Oil to cook
Preparation:

Dough:

Mix flour, salt and water together to make a soft dough (if the dough is hard add a little more water). I like mixing the dough by hand because I get a good feel for dryness or too wet a dough. If you accidentally add too much water, don't worry. Simply add a tbsp of flour and mix well. Knead the dough for a few minutes on a lightly greased surface to make a smooth and pliable dough. Set the dough aside and cover with a damp cloth. Let the dough rest for at least 20 minutes.

Filling:

Grate the cauliflower by hand. Heat 1 tbsp oil and add the spices and cook for about 45 seconds. Now add the chili and cauliflower along with the salt and cook on medium high heat till the cauliflower is cooked. Lastly, add the cilantro and keep aside to cool completely.

Making of parathas:

Divide the dough and cauliflower mixture into 6 equal parts. Roll the dough into 3-inch disks. Put the filling in the center. Seal by pulling the edges of the rolled dough together to make a ball. Proceed to make all six balls.

Each cauliflower filled ball needs to sit for two minutes before rolling. If you don't wait long enough the cauliflower mixture will seep through the edges when rolling the parathas.

Heat the cast iron skillet on medium high. To see if the skillet is ready, sprinkle a couple of drops of water on it. If the water sizzles rightt away, the skillet is ready. To make it easier to roll the balls, first roll them lightly in dry whole-wheat flour.

Lightly press the ball on the sealed side and keep it on the topside when rolling. Roll the ball light handed into 6-inch disks. To reduce chances of stickiness on the rolling pin or rolling surface, sprinkle small amounts of flour on both sides of the semi-rolled paratha.

Place the paratha over the skillet. You will see the color change on the bottom side and the paratha will bubble in different places.

Turn the paratha over. It should have golden-brown spots. Wait a few seconds and put 1 tsp of oil ove   r paratha and spread the oil on the topside. Flip the paratha and lightly press the puffed areas with a spatula. Flip again and press with the spatula making sure the paratha is golden-brown on both sides.

Cool the Parathas on a wire rack so they don't get soggy. Serve with any of the curries, chutneys and plain yogurt.

Chapattis

Yield: 8 chapattis

Ingredients:

1 cup whole-wheat pastry flour or spelt flour
1/4 tsp salt
1/2 cup hot water (Use more as needed)

Also needed:

2 tsp ghee
1/4 cup whole-wheat flour for rolling

Preparation:

Mix flour, salt and water together to make a soft dough (add more water as needed). Knead the dough on a lightly greased surface to make the dough smooth and pliable. Set the dough aside and cover with a damp cloth. Let the dough rest for 15 minutes. Divide the dough into 8 equal parts.

Make smooth ball and press flat. Take one ball; press it in the dry flour on both sides. Roll in to a 6-inch disk. If the dough sticks to the rolling pin or rolling surface, lightly dust the chapati with flour. *Make sure you only lightly dust the rolled chapati in the flour or else your end product will be too dry and stiff.* Heat the skillet on medium high heat. An iron skillet works best. To know if the skillet is hot enough, sprinkle few drops of water on the skillet. If the water sizzles immediately, the skillet is ready.

Place a rolled chapatti on the skillet. When it starts changing color and begins to puff up flip the bread over. Flip again after a few seconds. Take a flat spatula and press lightly on the puffed parts of the bread. This will help it puff up all over. Flip the bread again. It should have light golden-brown spots on both sides. Smear the bread with ghee and keep aside. Keep them in a container with a paper towel on the bottom.

Tip: make sure to cover the container after you put chapattis in it. This will keep the steam in and ensure the breads are soft. Serve with any of the curries in this book.

Indian cooking is fun, fragrant and colorful. A majority of these recipes are old and time-tested. I hope you feel a kinship with the people of India who have been cooking these dishes for many generations. At one time in history, spices were considered great wealth. The spices used in these recipes have a wealth of flavor and health benefits. Once you get a feel for it, you can explore and create your own recipes. Cook with your friends and family and celebrate life.

For more information about Aparna's books, food events and products, please visit: www.themistressofspice.com/blog

20310269R00034

Made in the USA
Charleston, SC
07 July 2013